BUSHEL
& PECK
BOOKS™

Published by Bushel & Peck Books, a family-run publishing house in Fresno, California, that believes in uplifting children with the highest standards of art, music, literature, and ideas. Find beautiful books for gifted young minds at www.bushelandpeckbooks.com.

Type set in Source Code Pro, Bobby Jones, and Futura.

"Tennis for Two" image sourced from Brookhaven National Laboratory via Wikimedia Commons; all other images and graphic elements licensed from the following Shutterstock.com artists: mhatzapa, WinWin artlab, Stakes, Kisho Van Tricht, isar braja, Lemonade Serenade, Gabi Krawczyk, Pablo Soria, Iriskana, JosepPerianes, ART PAL, HikaruD88, TeesArt, puruan, peace_art, Julia Tim, ReeFSubagja, Rijal fawwaz, Gohsantosa, Julia_Mak, Shamanistik_art, Red-Diamond, o_obolenskaya, Nikolaeva, wenchiawang, Costertoast, vivanm, Sailin on, Ed Connor, Alternative Publicidad, and Color Guru.

Designed by David Miles.
Edited by Emma Vetter.

All photographs and design elements licensed from Shutterstock.com.

Bushel & Peck Books is dedicated to fighting illiteracy all over the world. For every book we sell, we donate one to a child in need—book for book. To nominate a school or organization to receive free books, please visit www.bushelandpeckbooks.com.

ISBN: 9781638190998

First Edition

Printed in the United States

10 9 8 7 6 5 4 3 2 1

S.E. Abramson

THE SECRET LIVES OF VIDEO GAMES

The Remarkable
Stories Behind
the World's Most
Famous Video Games

CONTENTS

AUTHOR'S NOTE FOR PARENTS AND TEACHERS

Hello! Your child might have picked up this book because he or she wanted to learn more about today's popular video games. Or it could be that *you* wanted to learn about the games that your kids or students like to talk so much about. Let me give you a brief preview of what to expect.

What's In This Book

This book aims to be a resource that provides fun information—trivia facts; explanations about the history, genre, and story of a game; definitions of terms that experienced gamers understand but younger ones might not—in a way that is safe and friendly.

I have also included recommendations for kid-friendly YouTubers and Twitch streamers who play or make content about certain games. You can choose to use these at your own discretion, but I wanted you to at least be aware of them.

The games selected in this book are among the most popular games today or, if they're from the past, were significant milestones in the development of the video game industry. In every case, I've chosen to select games that are generally considered kid friendly and have ratings of either E (for Everyone) or T (for Teen). You'll find these ratings next to each game's introduction.

The Video Game Rating System

It might be helpful for you to have a brief overview of how video games are rated. The ESRB, or Entertainment Software Rating Board, rates games similarly to how the MPAA rates movies. Movies can be rated G, PG, PG-13, R, or NC-17 by the MPAA. The ESRB will rate games any of the following: E (Everyone, similar to a G-rated movie), E 10+ (Everyone 10+, similar to a PG rating), T (Teen 13+, similar to a PG-13 movie), M (Mature 17+, similar to an R rating), and AO (Adults Only 18+, similar to an X/NC-17 movie). Games that are being advertised but have not yet been released may have an RP (Rating Pending) or RP 17+ (Rating Pending 17+) rating. While the rating system is voluntary, most console manufacturers, U.S. game retailers, and mobile storefronts require ESRB ratings for every game they sell. The ESRB website offers more information about how to set up parental controls on consoles and computers in order to protect your child while still allowing them to experience the fun and joy of video games.

One point that should be noted is that AO games also include any games that use real currency to gamble—obviously, this is not a feature that movies have. Games with in-game currency and optional microtransactions do *not* receive an AO rating; they are instead given one of the other ratings as they do not use "real" currency. This is important because there are many popular games, such as *Raid: Shadow Legends* or *Genshin Impact*, which are mostly kid-friendly in terms of story and content (though they're not included in this book) but that do contain a form of gambling known as "gacha." If your child likes one of these games, it's important to monitor their game activity.

Enjoy!

With all that, I hope you and your child or student enjoys this book! If they're passionate about video games, *you* learning more about gaming can give you a wonderful way to connect. Happy reading, and happy gaming!

—S. E. Abramson

THE FIRST COMPUTER GAME

"BERTIE THE BRAIN"

NO ESRB RATING

Tic-Tac-Toe is a simple game that most people learn to play on pen and paper. However, it was also the model for the first video game ever created.

In the year 1950, a radio company called Rogers Majestic asked one of their employees, Dr. Josef Kates, to create a display for the Canadian National Exhibition. Dr. Kates got to work and built "Bertie the Brain," a computer that was nearly thirteen feet tall! Today, some people might argue that Bertie wasn't a real video game because it didn't have an electronic screen or video. However, there were buttons to press and parts of the machine that lit up—and most importantly, Bertie was a computer.

For two weeks at the Canadian National Exhibition, attendees could line up to play a game of Tic-Tac-Toe with Bertie. Dr. Kates stayed with Bertie through most of the exhibition so that he could adjust how difficult the game was for each challenger. Bertie was a huge success at the Exhibition—even comedian Danny Kaye played a few rounds!

THE FIRST "VIDEO" GAME

TENNIS FOR TWO

NO ESRB RATING

ust like Bertie the Brain, the first video game that used a video screen was also invented by a scientist. William Higinbottom was a physicist who worked for Brookhaven National Laboratory in Upton, New York. Brookhaven National Laboratory held annual visitor's days, during which thousands of people often came to tour the lab and see what happened there. Higinbottom noticed that a lot of the visitors seemed to be bored with the displays and decided that he wanted to make something interactive.

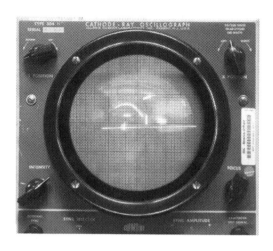

Can you make out the tennis "ball" on the screen to the left?

The laboratory owned a small analog computer that could show things like a ball of light bouncing from side to side. Higinbottom was inspired by this computer to make a tennis game, and thus *Tennis for Two* was born. A technician named Robert Dvorak helped Higinbottom to build a new analog computer with dials that could be turned to adjust the angle of the ball and buttons that were pressed to hit the ball. There were two simple lines on the screen: one for the ground and one for the net. It looked like a tennis court from the side.

Tennis for Two was first shown off on the laboratory visitor's day in 1958. The visitors absolutely *loved* the game, to the point where the display was reused the following year. Higinbottom did add a couple of quality-of-life changes: a bigger display screen and the ability for the game to simulate different levels of gravity. Imagine being able to play tennis on the moon!

1958

COMPUTER SPACE

FIGHTING OFF THE FIRST ENEMIES

NO ESRB RATING

Though Bertie the Brain and *Tennis for Two* were created in the 1950s, video games weren't made for commercial use until the 1970s—and it only happened because of arcades.

If you've ever been to a Chuck-E-Cheese or an amusement park arcade, you've probably seen all kinds of games there—both video and mechanical games. During the 1960s, arcades had claw machines and basketball hoops. However, in 1971, video games were introduced to arcades for the first time.

Two electrical engineers named Nolan Bushnell and Ted Dabney formed a company known as Sygyzy Engineering. (*Sygyzy* means the alignment of planets in space.) They created a game called *Computer Space*. In *Computer Space*, the player controls a flying rocket while also fighting off two AI-controlled flying saucers.

Computer Space achieved some success in arcades between 1971 and 1972. The machine was designed to charge ten cents per game or three games for a quarter. The lines to play the game at arcades were usually at least ten people long.

Bushnell and Dabney went on to incorporate Sygyzy into a new company that may sound familiar: Atari, Inc. They launched *Pong* in 1972—which would have looked familiar to anybody who had played *Tennis for Two* at the Brookhaven National Laboratory open house, as it was also a tennis-style game.

Pong became the first commercially successful video game. But even though it started out as an arcade game, it would also pave the way for the future—console games.

PAC-MAN

A MEMORABLE MUNCHING MONSTER

RATED E FOR EVERYONE

ven if you've never played *Pac-Man*, you've probably seen the characters or heard the music at some point in your life. Pac-Man is a small yellow fellow shaped like a pizza with one slice missing. And his four enemies are pixel ghosts: Blinky, Pinky, Inky, and Clyde.

In 1974, Japanese video game development company Namco acquired the Japanese division of Atari (yes, the same Atari that created *Computer Space* and *Pong*). In 1979, one of the employees, Toru Iwatani, wanted to create a non-violent, cheerful video game that would encourage arcades to

DID YOU KNOW?

Each of the four ghosts was programmed to have a different personality. Some are more aggressive, while others are more stealthy.

serve as family-friendly environments. He decided to focus his game on eating: Pac-Man's goal would be to eat all of the pellets in the maze without being eaten by the ghosts.

Pac-Man took a year and five months to make—this was the longest development period so far for any game in the world! Testing for the game began in 1980, and the play-testers liked the game a lot. Pac-Man was Japan's fourth highest-grossing arcade game of 1981—and, in America, it was the highest-grossing arcade game. It even surpassed the film Star Wars: A New Hope, earning more than one billion dollars. Pac-Man is considered to be one of the most influential video games of all time.

1984

··TETRIS

A CLASSIC PUZZLE
GAME WITH A
COMPLICATED
HISTORY

RATED E FOR EVERYONE

ven if you haven't made the connection of the name *Tetris* to the visual image of the game, you probably know what it is. A classic *Tetris* game screen features falling tetrominoes (shapes created with different combinations of four squares), which you must line up and complete rows with in order to cause them to disappear and create more room on the screen. The disappearing rows grant the player points, and the game ends when no more space can be filled. Tetris was created in 1984 by software engineer Alexey Pajitnov, and it was instantly successful. It's been around in the world's pop-culture consciousness practically since it was created, to the point where people often make jokes about "fridge Tetris" or "dishwasher Tetris" as a way of saying it's sometimes a struggle to fit all the food in the fridge or all of the dishes in the dishwasher

But while the game was successful, Pajitnov didn't always get the credit he deserved for inventing the game. Pajitnov was from Russia—or, as it was known in 1984, the Soviet Union.

His job was to test the capabilities of speech recognition hardware, but Pajitnov's ambition was to use computers to make

people happy. Once he had finished making *Tetris*, it proved to be almost too successful: he showed it to his fellow employees at work, and all of them were *very* distracted from their jobs because of the game. Pajitnov recruited Vadim Gerasimov, a 16-year-old high school student, to help him code and adapt it for the IBM Personal Computer.

Pajitnov didn't really know how the business world worked, but he wanted to share *Tetris* with the world. There were a few problems with this: the Soviet Union was a Communist country and had a law stating that intellectual property did not exist. That meant that Pajitnov legally wasn't allowed to make any money from his game.

Eventually, word got around. In 1986, Pajitnov's supervisor at his job sent a copy of *Tetris* to a Hungarian game publisher called Novotrade. The game began to spread around Eastern Europe and even caught the eye of a business-man named Robert Stein, a salesman for Andromeda Software located in London.

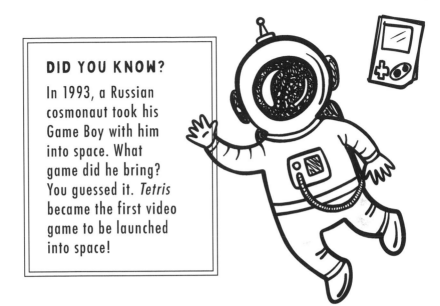

DID YOU KNOW?

In 1993, a Russian cosmonaut took his Game Boy with him into space. What game did he bring? You guessed it. *Tetris* became the first video game to be launched into space!

Stein contacted Pajitnov to obtain the licensing rights to Tetris. Pajitnov expressed interest in forming an agreement, but they didn't know that Stein took this as a legal contract and promptly began approaching companies to produce the game, technically trying to sell a game he didn't properly own.

He was eventually forced to work with Elektronorgtechnica, or "Elorg" for short, the Soviet Union's government organization for the import and export of computer software. Stein and Elorg eventually came to an agreement, signing a ten-year contract. Elorg requested 80% of the revenue, and Pajitnov would not get any of it because of the laws surrounding intellectual property. It all grew into a huge legal mess, and Stein simply... didn't mention the companies who were *already* producing the game to Elorg. This was very, *very* illegal, and it was making Stein a lot of money that he wasn't telling Elorg about. At one point, about twelve companies believed that they owned the rights to Tetris, though Stein retained the rights for the home computer version.

A Dutch video game designer named Henk Rogers attempted to get the hand-held console rights for *Tetris* from Atari—and, in the process, uncovered Stein's deception of and breach of contract with Elorg. He promptly exposed Stein to Elorg and properly obtained the rights for handheld console versions of *Tetris* on behalf of Nintendo. Nintendo sued Atari and the other companies who were producing *Tetris* games, and the courts ruled in their favor.

After the dissolution of the Soviet

Union, Elorg became a private business instead of a government organization. Rogers had arranged things so that the rights for the game would revert to Pajitnov, who moved to the United States in 1991. Together, Rogers and Pajitnov founded The Tetris Company in 1996, and have since owned all rights to the *Tetris* brand.

Tetris is the most ported video game in history, appearing on over 65 different platforms. It is the most successful non-Nintendo game in the world (as the agreement with Nintendo expired before 1996).

When Pajitnov turned *Tetris* into a proper game, he got help from Vadim Gerasimov, who was only sixteen years old but already well-known for his coding skills. Did you know that there are a lot of resources available for you to learn how to code? There are all kinds of online programs and games that will teach you how. You could even learn to code using Roblox. And maybe someday, you can code your own video game!

SUPER MARIO BROS.

IT'S-A-ME, THE MOST FAMOUS VIDEO GAME CHARACTER IN THE WORLD

RATED E FOR EVERYONE

If you had to ask anyone in the world about the first video game that popped into their head, it's almost guaranteed that most of them would say "Mario," or "Super Mario." Why is that? Well, it's hard not to know who Mario is when he and his games have been so successful throughout video game history—*and* when he's the official mascot of Nintendo!

The Mario franchise as a whole has sold over seven hundred and seventy million games. These range from the *Super Mario* games to *Mario Party*, *Mario Sports*, *Mario Kart*, and so on. It is the best-selling video game franchise of all time and has been successful in other media including three animated television series, some comic books, a manga, and other merchandise.

The original *Mario Bros.* games were made just for the arcades and designed to be enjoyed in multiplayer. Mario and Luigi exterminate creatures emerging from the sewers by knocking them upside-down and kicking them away. In most future *Super Mario Bros.* releases, the original *Mario Bros.* game has been available as a mini-game.

Nintendo developers Shigeru Miyamoto and Takashi Tezuka then went on to create the *Super Mario Bros.* games, designed for home consoles. The very first game, simply titled *Super Mario Bros.*, was

DID YOU KNOW?
Mario and Luigi are based on plumbers! That's why they wear overalls and why the famous green pipes appear in nearly all of the games. Even though Luigi is taller than Mario, Mario is the older of the two brothers. They are actually twin brothers—and the height difference means that they would be fraternal twins instead of identical twins.

DID YOU KNOW?

Mario was named after Mario Segale, the man who owned the land where Nintendo of America's offices were built. In 2015, Nintendo officials stated that Mario's last name is also Mario, so his full name is . . . Mario Mario. (And yes, that means that Luigi's full name is Luigi Mario.)

released for the Nintendo Entertainment System (NES) in 1985. *Super Mario Bros.* introduces the classic elements of the *Mario* series, such as the plot (Princess Peach is kidnapped by Bowser, and Mario must save her), the enemies (Goombas and Koopa Troopas), and the power-ups (Super Mushroom, Fire Flower, and Super Star). The game has eight worlds with four levels in each world, making for a total of thirty-two levels in the game. The fourth level in every world is always a fortress or a castle, and the level always ends with a fight against Bowser or one of his minions. This sets the player up to believe they are finding Princess Peach in worlds one through seven—but they only find the character Toad, who informs them: "Thank you Mario! But our princess is in another castle!"

The games in the Mario series include:

- *Super Mario Bros. (1985)*
- *Super Mario Bros.: The Lost Levels (1986)*
- *Super Mario Bros. 2 (1988)*
- *Super Mario Bros. 3 (1988)*
- *Super Mario Land (1989)*
- *Super Mario World (1990)*
- *Super Mario Land 2: 6 Golden Coins (1992)*
- *Super Mario World 2: Yoshi's Island (1995)*
- *Super Mario 64 (1996)*
- *Super Mario Sunshine (2002)*
- *New Super Mario*

DID YOU KNOW?

Mario has a mustache because he was originally an 8-bit character, and it's hard to make a nose or mouth show up on an 8-bit character unless there's something nearby that shows off the shape of those features. This is also true for other parts of Mario's appearance—they couldn't design hair or ears very well, so he has a hat and sideburns instead.

Bros. (2006)
- *Super Mario Galaxy (2007)*
- *New Super Mario Bros. Wii (2009)*
- *Super Mario Galaxy 2 (2010)*
- *Super Mario 3D Land (2011)*
- *New Super Mario Bros. 2 (2012)*
- *New Super Mario Bros. U (2012)*
- *Super Mario 3D World (2013)*
- *Super Mario Maker (2015)*
- *Super Mario Run (2016)*
- *Super Mario Odyssey (2017)*
- *Super Mario Maker 2 (2019)*
- *Super Mario 3D World + Bowser's Fury (2021)*

And that's *just* the main series games.

THE LEGEND OF ZELDA

A TIMELESS(?) TALE OF A COURAGEOUS HERO

RATED E10+ FOR EVERYONE 10+

In recent years, it's become popular for video game heroes to struggle with moral choices. People like to read about and play as characters who have to deal with making tough decisions, similar to the ones they need to make in their own lives. However, this sometimes

---

DID YOU KNOW?

The Legend of Zelda was partially based on creator Shigeru Miyamoto's childhood experiences exploring the woods and caves of Sonobe, Japan. He wanted to recreate that feeling of exploration in the game! Miyamoto has actually helped create a lot of Nintendo game series, from Mario to Pikmin to Starfox.

---

means that heroes seem bad, and villains seem good—and sometimes this makes a great story, but sometimes it's just confusing.

The Legend of Zelda, in this sense, has always been very clear about the roles of heroes and villains. The main character, Link, is a hero; he receives guidance from Zelda, the princess; and he works to defeat the villain, who is usually Ganon. Even though it's a simple formula, it works every time. *The Legend of Zelda* series has been popular since it was introduced to the world in 1986—and with the massive success of the Nintendo Switch's 2017 launch game, *The Legend of Zelda: Breath of the Wild*, it's not going anywhere any time soon.

Some of the games, such as the very first title *The Legend of Zelda*, are very simple adventures— find weapons and items, then fight the bad guys. Some use complex dynamics, such as the ability to become two-dimensional at will in *The Legend of Zelda: A Link Between Worlds* or the ability to shrink down to a very small size in *The Legend of Zelda: The Minish Cap*.

What all games have in common, however, is puzzle-solving. The puzzles vary between games, but each game relies on its own unique dynamics in order to solve puzzles. For instance: in *The Legend of Zelda: Oracle*

DID YOU KNOW?

Speaking of Mario and Zelda in the same game, *The Legend of Zelda: Link's Awakening* has a lot, and we do mean A LOT, of Mario enemies. From Madame Meowmeow's pet Chain Chomp to the Goombas you can find just about anywhere, it's a wonderland of references and Easter eggs.

DID YOU KNOW?

In *The Legend of Zelda: Breath of the Wild*, Nintendo made some sound effects for some very . . . interesting animations. If you sneak up on a Bokoblin and watch it for a while without it knowing you're there, at some point it's going to start picking its nose. If you listen closely, you can actually hear it—kind of gross, but also pretty cool. One of the sound directors of Breath of the Wild said that they made the noise by sticking a finger in a wet cloth and squishing it around close to the recording microphone.

of *Seasons*, Link gets an item called the Rod of Seasons. With this rod, he has the ability to hop up onto tree stumps and wave the wand to change the season to spring, summer, fall, or winter. Different puzzles must be solved in different seasons—some areas can only be accessed in winter when the water has iced over; some can only be accessed in spring when certain flowers bloom (and even shoot Link to new places). Some areas can only be accessed in fall when you can pick mushrooms that block your path during all other seasons. As Link gains access to each of the different seasons, he is able to travel to new places on the map, solve more puzzles, and progress further in his quest. Many of the *Legend of Zelda* games are stylized in this way.

The *Legend of Zelda* series is also known for its remarkable music. Even if you have never played a *Legend of Zelda* game, you've probably heard either the "Hyrule Field Theme," "Song of Storms," or "Zelda's Lullaby." In particular, *The Legend of Zelda: The Ocarina of Time* introduced a musical mechanic to the game whereby Link must solve puzzles by playing short songs on an ocarina, which is a small ceramic flute. Similarly, in the 3DS title *The Legend of Zelda: Spirit Tracks*, Link solves similar puzzles by playing a pan flute—which the player does by blowing into the 3DS microphone! Not every game in the series has used the musical motif, but most of them have music that a player would recognize from a previous title.

Behind the stories of each individual game is one overarching story which the fanbase refers to as "the timeline." The games don't always act as direct sequels to previous games; in fact, each game can be played as more or less a standalone adventure, and you don't need to have played one game to succeed at another. However, all of the games are connected and take place in the same universe. It's a complicated timeline, but Nintendo released a book in 2013 called *The Legend of Zelda: Hyrule Historia* which explains the chronological story order of the games. The developers have also clarified where games released since 2013 fall within this timeline, so you'll be able to understand where your favorite *Legend of Zelda* game fits into the wider *Legend of Zelda* lore.

METROID

"HEY, WOULDN'T THAT BE KIND OF COOL IF IT TURNED OUT THE PERSON IN THIS SUIT WAS A WOMAN?"

**SOME RATED E FOR EVERYONE;
SOME RATED E10+ FOR EVERYONE 10+;
SOME RATED T FOR TEEN**

While the first *Metroid* game was in development, one of the developers asked the above question—and a legacy was born.

In the *Metroid* series, you play as bounty hunter Samus Aran. She wears a super cool mecha-suit (so she looks more like a robot than a person, most of the time) to protect the galaxy from Space Pirates and other threats, and she works to prevent them from using the power of Metroid parasites.

It's such a simple thing, but in

1986 (when the first *Metroid* game was released), there were barely any mainstream video games with a female protagonist. Many people became interested in the games because Samus was a girl but not just a damsel in distress: she was cool, clever, and powerful, and she was the hero of the games. The developers took inspiration from Ridley Scott's 1979 sci-fi horror film *Alien*, which also features a female protagonist. In fact, they were so inspired that one of the main antagonists of the first game, and thereafter the series, was even named Ridley.

From 1986 to 2000, the *Metroid* games were two-dimensional, side-scrolling games, much like the original *Super Mario Bros*. In fact, *Metroid* games became known for this style of gameplay, as well as the concept of an open-world platformer—meaning that players would have to backtrack to places they had already been to access certain areas once they had the abilities necessary to reach them. Along with another game well-known for this gameplay style, the *Castlevania* games, this type of game became known in both the video game industry and the gaming community as "Metroidvania," which is a term used even today to refer to two-dimensional, side-scrolling open-world platformer games. Games such as *Hollow Knight, Ori and the Blind Forest,* the *Shantae* series, *MegaMan,* and *Dead Cells* are all considered Metroidvanias.

Metroid, the first game, was released in 1986 for the Nintendo Famicom System. It was followed by *Metroid II: Return of Samus* in 1991 for the Game Boy System. *Super Metroid,* for the SNES, was released in 1994. *Metroid Fusion* in 2002 and *Zero Mission,* a 2004 remake of the original *Metroid,* were next. All five of these games were successful.

After 2000, Nintendo explored the idea of turning the *Metroid* series into three-dimensional games. In 2002 they released *Metroid Prime*, a 3D game for the GameCube with a first-person perspective; the sequels *Metroid Prime 2: Echoes* in 2004 and *Metroid Prime 3: Corruption* in 2007 (on the Nintendo Wii) followed. These games also did fairly well, but unfortunately, the 2010 release of *Metroid: Other M* didn't sell well. Fans of the series disliked both how Samus was written in this game and the reduced focus on exploration that was a staple of all the other games thus far. After a Metroid-themed minigame in the 2012 release *Nintendo Land*, Nintendo published *Metroid Prime: Federation Force* for the 3DS in 2016, which was also a failure.

Fortunately, in 2017, Nintendo decided to return to Metroid's 2D, side-scrolling roots with a remake of *Metroid II* for the 3DS. *Metroid: Samus Returns* retained 3D graphics while going back to the original feel of the *Metroid* series, and the game was successful with fans. Most recently, *Metroid Dread* (originally a Nintendo DS project, planned to be released in 2006 but ultimately canceled) was released for the Nintendo Switch in 2021. It sold over 2.9 million copies by May 2022 and is the best-selling *Metroid* game of all time.

Samus is also a playable character in all five of the *Super Smash Bros.* fighting games, with Zero Suit Samus being added in *Super Smash Bros: Brawl* and Dark Samus and Ridley being added in *Super Smash Bros: Ultimate*.

SONIC THE HEDGEHOG

GOTTA GO FAST

MOST RATED E FOR EVERYONE; SOME RATED E10+ FOR EVERYONE 10+

During the massive growth of video game companies in the late 1980s, 1990s, and 2000s, Nintendo was king—but they were not without their competitors for the throne. The Japanese company Sega created Sonic the Hedgehog in his very first game in 1991, conceiving him as competition for Nintendo's mascot, Mario. Both the Mario games and the *Sonic* games are platformers; and, similarly to Mario, the *Sonic* games developed spin-offs in different genres such as racing, fighting, and sports.

The story of the series typically follows

DID YOU KNOW?

The game designers at Sega came up with several ideas for a mascot character to rival Nintendo's Mario. The main designer, Naoto Ohshima, took some of the ideas with him on a trip to New York City and asked random passersby in Central Park their opinions about which one they thought would look cool as a video game character. Some of the designs included an armadillo, a dog, a rabbit with long ears, and a guy in pajamas; but the most popular vote went to a hedgehog design. When Mr. Ohshima took the designs back to Japan, the research department voted unanimously to select the hedgehog as the new mascot. (The "guy in pajamas" design would later become Sonic's enemy, Dr. Eggman!)

Sonic, a blue hedgehog who battles Doctor Eggman. Usually, gameplay involves traversing dangerous worlds, collecting rings, and running around loop-de-loops. Later games added well-known characters such as Tails, Knuckles, and Shadow (and many, many more). Sega would later allow the *Sonic* games to cross over with other video game franchises in games like the *Mario & Sonic* series, *Sega All-Stars*, and *Super Smash Bros.*

Though the *Sonic* games are frequently criticized for a lack of quality and cohesive gameplay, they are still important to the video game industry and are often referenced in pop culture.

Did you know that there are over ninety games in the *Sonic* franchise? These include the main series 2D platformers, 3D games, racing games, and crossover games, among other things.

DID YOU KNOW?

Sonic is blue because the Sega logo is blue, but his red and white shoes were inspired by both Michael Jackson (specifically from the 1987 album *Bad*) and Santa Claus. His personality was based, oddly enough, on at-the-time United States presidential candidate and later US president Bill Clinton.

DID YOU KNOW?

Game designer Yuji Naka believed the common misconception that hedgehogs were incapable of swimming, so he decided that Sonic wouldn't be able to swim. In just about every water-themed level in the Sonic games, he either wears a life jacket or has to avoid water entirely. (As it turns out, hedgehogs can swim! Some of them don't like to swim very much, but they do know how and are actually quite good at it because their quills are filled with air to help keep them afloat.)

FIFA

IT'S OFFICIAL

RATED E FOR EVERYONE

As of 2021, the *FIFA* series has sold over 325 million copies. It is the best-selling sports video game franchise in the world and is available in 18 languages and 51 countries.

What makes it so popular? The answer is simple: it's about the most popular sport in the world—football (or soccer, if you're American). The *FIFA* games are licensed by and named after the real-world organization FIFA, the world's governing body of football. FIFA is a French acronym, standing for *Fédération Internationale de Football Association.* (In English, it's called the International Federation of Association Football, but FIFA is a little more catchy than IFAF, don't you think?)

One of *FIFA*'s many draws is the ability to play as your favorite teams and players. The games in the series date back to the 1990s, so if you weren't satisfied with how well your team did in the real-life world championship in any particular year—then hey, you can pretend *it never happened*. You can also build your own teams, putting together your favorite players who might never play on the same team in real life.

Interested in *FIFA*? You can probably play it on *any* device you have. From the ancient Sega Genesis to the PlayStation 5, Nintendo Switch, Xbox Series X, iOS, and Windows—there are games for pretty much every system out there. Make sure you have parental permission before buying or downloading any games!

POKÉMON

GOTTA CATCH 'EM ALL

RATED E FOR EVERYONE

In 1996, game developer Satoshi Tajiri created the first *Pokémon* games: *Pokémon Red* and *Pokémon Green*. The games are centered around fictional creatures known as Pokémon. Humans catch and train Pokémon to battle with one another. Pokémon is an abbreviation for "Pocket Monsters," a reference to the fact that a Poké Ball can fit comfortably in the palm of one's hand. The games were published for Nintendo's handheld Game Boy system in February 1996.

Over the years, the *Pokémon* game regions have been based on real-world geographical locations. These include different parts of Japan, New York

City, France, Hawaii, and the United Kingdom. References to these real-world locations are made in-game through the names of Pokémon, cities, and items. For example, in *Pokémon Sun* and *Pokémon Moon*, the games are set in the fictional region of Alola, which is based upon Hawaii. References to Hawaii include characters greeting one another by saying "Alola!" which sounds similar to "Aloha!" and the presence of a food item known as "malasadas," which are a Portuguese treat similar to donuts that have grown popular in Hawaii throughout the years.

With only a few exceptions, there have been *Pokémon* games released nearly every year since 1996. They are as follows:

- *Pokémon Red and Pokémon Green: February 27, 1996 (Japan), September 28, 1998 (North America)*
- *Pokémon Blue: October 10, 1996 (JP)*

DID YOU KNOW?

Many of the English names for Pokémon are puns! Here are some examples:

- Mimikyu sounds like "mimic you," and since its appearance suggests that it's really trying to look a lot like a Pikachu, that's pretty much on the nose.
- Squirtle is a turtle that can squirt you with water. Squirt + turtle = Squirtle.
- Sudowoodo looks like a tree...but it's actually a Rock-type Pokémon. The word "pseudo," which is pronounced like "sudo," means false. So Sudowoodo means "false wood," which makes perfect sense because Sudowoodo isn't really a tree; it's a rock. (It's actually petrified wood, which means that it used to be a tree a very long time ago, but at this point, it is actually now a rock. If you want to learn more about petrified wood, you can research in your school library or with the help of Google!)

DID YOU KNOW?

The Pacific Island nation of Niue has put Pikachu (and a few other Pokémon) on some of their dollar coins! Niue mostly uses the New Zealand Dollar (NZD) for their money, but the Pokémon coins are also accepted as legal tender—meaning they are real money. Imagine buying a snack or a toy with money that has Pikachu on it!

- *Pokémon Yellow: September 12, 1998 (JP), October 19, 1999 (NA)*
- *Pokémon Gold and Pokémon Silver: November 21, 1999 (JP), October 15, 2000 (NA)*
- *Pokémon Crystal: December 14, 2000 (JP), July 29, 2001 (NA)*
- *Pokémon Ruby and Pokémon Sapphire: November 21, 2002 (JP), March 19, 2003 (NA)*
- *Pokémon FireRed and Pokémon LeafGreen: January 29, 2004 (JP), September 9, 2004 (NA)*
- *Pokémon Emerald: September 16, 2004 (JP), May 1, 2005 (NA)*
- *Pokémon Diamond and Pokémon Pearl: September 28, 2006 (JP), April 22, 2007 (NA)*

- *Pokémon Platinum:* September 13, 2008 (JP), March 22, 2009 (NA)
- *Pokémon HeartGold and Pokémon SoulSilver:* September 12, 2009 (JP), March 14, 2010 (NA)
- *Pokémon Black and Pokémon White:* September 18, 2010 (JP), March 6, 2011 (NA)
- *Pokémon Black 2 and Pokémon White 2:* June 23, 2012 (JP), October 7, 2012 (NA)
- *Pokémon X and Pokémon Y:* October 12, 2013
- *Pokémon Omega Ruby and Pokémon Alpha Sapphire:* November 21, 2014
- *Pokémon Sun and Pokémon Moon:* November 18, 2016
- *Pokémon Ultra Sun and Pokémon Ultra Moon:* November 17, 2017
- *Pokémon: Let's Go, Pikachu and Pokémon: Let's Go Eevee:* November 16, 2018
- *Pokémon Sword and Pokémon Shield:* November 15, 2019
- *Pokémon Brilliant Diamond and Pokémon Shining Pearl:* November 19, 2021
- *Pokémon Legends: Arceus:* January

28, 2022
- *Pokémon Scarlet and Pokémon Violet: TBD— Fall 2022*

In addition to the main Pokémon games, there have also been *Pokémon Rangers* games, *Pokémon Mystery Dungeon* games, and of course the massively popular mobile game, *Pokémon Go*.

Beyond the games, there are also the anime and manga series, over twenty animated movies, trading cards, and even plushies. *Pokémon* is largely considered to be one of the most successful video game franchises of all time.

DID YOU KNOW?

Many Pokémon are based on Japanese folklore and legends about scary monsters—but once you've caught one to use on your team, they don't seem very scary, do they? Lotad, Lombre, and Ludicolo are based on the kappa, a demon who holds water on its head— but honestly, who could be scared of these little guys? Vulpix and Ninetales are based on the kitsune, a many-tailed fox spirit whose power grows as they become older and wiser. "Kitsune" simply means "fox" in Japanese, but in English, the word refers specifically to the legendary fox spirit.

DID YOU KNOW?

As the Pokémon games have grown in popularity around the world, some of them are now based on legends and myths from other countries as well! Many Pokémon fans were surprised when their floppy, adorable Magikarp evolved into powerful blue dragon Gyarados. The two didn't seem to have anything in common. But Magikarp and Gyarados are actually based on a Chinese story called "Dragon Gate." In this story, the Dragon Gate sits at the top of a tall waterfall, and any carp that are able to leap their way up to the top of the waterfall are rewarded by transforming into dragons. How cool is that?

Did you know that you can trade Pokémon with your friends online? In the earliest days of *Pokémon* games, you would link your Game Boy systems with a physical wire known as a Link Cable. The Nintendo DS was able to make use of local wireless signals to trade with nearby friends, while the 3DS introduced the internet and an online trading system, which has continued through with the Nintendo Switch. Just beware of hackers—if that level 100 shiny Charizard seems too good to be true, it probably is.

ANIMAL CROSSING

DESIGN YOUR OWN
HOME AND BEFRIEND
ANIMAL VILLAGERS

RATED E FOR EVERYONE

There may only be five games in the *Animal Crossing* series, but boy, are those games good. If you ever wanted to play a game to just relax, to not worry about anything or even get caught up in a story, then *Animal Crossing* is where it's at.

In *Animal Crossing*, you play as a human who lives in a village with animal villagers. You can go fishing, catch bugs, and dig up fossils to complete a magnificent museum; but you can also sell your finds to Tom Nook, a tanuki (a magical raccoon-like creature of Japanese myth) who owns the village store in every *Animal Crossing* game. (He also, by way of running the real estate market in the game, owns your soul. Please, Mr. Nook...I just want to pay off my house...)

...ahem. Speaking of houses, you can purchase one, upgrade it to include more rooms, and decorate it to your heart's content with furniture, rugs, and wallpaper that you can buy at the store (or in more recent games, craft out of gathered resources like sticks and stones).

In addition to your home and the town's museum, the other game objectives generally include things like making your town look pretty by planting flowers and trees, cleaning up trash and seashells from the beaches, and befriending the villagers who come to live in your town. But there's no stress and no pressure to complete these tasks. The game allows you to play at your own pace, on your own time. Where many games constantly remind you that you need to complete this quest or collect these items, *Animal Crossing* just lets you *play*.

The villagers are a huge part of the game. As you play, they will come to live in your village and provide you with friendship and sometimes even presents. And with a roster of nearly four hundred villagers as of the most recent game, *Animal Crossing: New Horizons*, there are plenty of them to befriend.

Animal Crossing was released in 2001 to great success. It was followed by *Animal Crossing: Wild World* (2005); *Animal Crossing: City Folk* (2008); *Animal Crossing: New Leaf* (2012); and *Animal Crossing: New Horizons* (2020). There have also been several spin-off games such as

---

DID YOU KNOW?

In older *Animal Crossing* games, the villagers could sometimes be a little bit mean to you if you annoyed them enough—pushing them around, hitting them with your net, and so on. Some of them will even insult you, saying things like "I'm going to have to come up with something nice to say about you that's believable," or "I hope you get stung by a thousand bees." In newer games, they become angry if you do those things, but they won't insult you anymore.

DID YOU KNOW?

An interesting feature of the Animal Crossing games is that it uses the real-world clock and calendar to simulate the passage of time. If you play during the day, it will be daytime in the game; if you play at night, it will be night in the game. If you play in January, there will be snow on the ground—and if you play in October, the trees will have red and orange leaves. Animal Crossing: New Horizons even adds support for northern and southern hemisphere seasons, so that players who live in, say, Australia can have summer in December and winter in June, just how they're used to it in real life. The game also has in-game holidays that imitate real ones—for example, "Toy Day" for Christmas and "Bunny Day" for Easter.

Happy Home Designer (2015) and the popular mobile version, *Pocket Camp* (2017). In *New Leaf*, the player is elected as the mayor and allowed to make major changes to the topography of the town such as adding bridges and public works like fountains and campsites. *New Horizons* takes customization a step further and allows the player the ability to terraform their island. Have you ever wanted to re-route a river, like Luisa from *Encanto*? In *New Horizons*, you can do that *with your phone*.

Animal Crossing multiplayer mode allows other players of the game to use an Internet connection on their Nintendo Switch to visit your island in *New Horizons* if they have the right password. Be careful about allowing strangers onto your island—always practice internet safety!

ROBLOX

OOF

RATED E10+ FOR EVERYONE 10+

ven if you've never played *Roblox*, you probably know the "*Roblox* death sound," as it's used in many comedic animations and memes. *Roblox*'s "OOF" noise is an iconic sound sample of the 2010s.

But that's not all that *Roblox* is known for. *Roblox* is an online game platform and game creation system.

DID YOU KNOW?

The classic "oof" death noise that has made Roblox so famous over the years can change in sound based on the speed of the Humanoid at the time of its death. If your Humanoid is moving fast enough, the sound's going to come out very different!

If you're interested in coding and looking around in the game files, you can actually find that sound file. It's named "uuuuh.wav."

It allows the users to create their own games and play games made by other users.

Roblox was created by David Baszucki and Eric Cassel in 2004. Over the years, the game went from simply a block-building game similar to *Minecraft* to a game that allowed users to learn the basics of coding and game development within the coding language of *Roblox*'s platform.

Some of the most popular games created on *Roblox* include *Adopt Me!*, *Break In*, *Jailbreak*, *MeepCity*, *Murder Mystery 2*, *Natural Disaster Survival*, *Phantom Forces*, *Piggy*, *Royale High*, *Welcome to Bloxburg*, and *Work at a Pizza Place*. The games encourage socialization and

DID YOU KNOW?

Lua is the name of the coding language used by both the official game developers and the players who design their own games within Roblox Studio. Lua is a recognized coding language just like Java, Python, or C. If you've ever designed something in Roblox, you're well on your way to becoming a computer programmer or a game designer!

cooperation with other players.

In July 2020, *Roblox* introduced a feature called "Party Place," which functions as an online hangout. It was designed in response to the COVID-19 pandemic so that kids who enjoy *Roblox* would be able to hang out with their friends while playing the game. Some people have even celebrated their birthday parties on *Roblox*!

It's important to remember Internet safety when you play any game online, whether it's *Roblox*, *Minecraft*, or any other MMO. You should never give out your personal or financial information to anyone you meet online. And you should never ask anyone for their personal or financial information, so you can help others to be safe as well.

PORTAL

THE CAKE IS A LIE /////////

SOME RATED E FOR EVERYONE;
SOME RATED E10+ FOR EVERYONE 10+;
SOME RATED T FOR TEEN

I n October 2007, video game developers Valve released a short game called *Portal* as part of "The Orange Box," which was a compilation of a few of their other games, including *Half-Life 2* and *Team Fortress 2*. Valve initially thought of *Portal* as a bonus feature to accompany the deal with the two other games that were (at the time) much more popular. This might have been because the game concept was originally developed by a group of students from the DigiPen Institute of Technology and show-cased at a career fair. Valve saw the game (originally named *Narbacular Drop*) and offered the entire group of students jobs to further develop the game. So, of course, *Portal* was a little bonus project, an experimental feature included as a treat for players who purchased "The Orange Box."

Oh, how wrong they were. *Portal* was an instant success, for several reasons: it was funny (if occasionally a touch morbid), it had a unique game mechanic, and it had a great physics engine.

The gameplay for *Portal* is fairly simple. You play as Chell, a human being guided through a series of "experimental test chambers" by GLaDOS, a robot AI. At the beginning of the game, Chell receives the "Aperture Science Handheld Portal Device," or as most players call it, the portal gun. The portal gun creates a human-sized wormhole between two flat surfaces, allowing the player to walk or fall into one and emerge from the other—even if they are on opposite sides of the room. An important feature of the portals is that the player's momentum is preserved when they move through the portals, and this makes it possible for

DID YOU KNOW?

"The cake is a lie" was a popular meme/catchphrase in the 2010s, and it's still carried through today. It originated from GLaDOS telling the player that, if they complete the next experiment, they will be given cake. This happens after each experiment and yet... no cake. Later, the player sees sentences written on a wall that say, "the cake is a lie" over and over. Basically, the cake thing became a recurring line throughout the game and in fan communities, and it later became popular enough to be used by people who had never even played the game. So, if you're promised a reward that never actually comes, you can always say "the cake is a lie."

the player to jump to very great heights using the power of gravity.

With the occasional hint or explanation, GLaDOS guides Chell through test chamber after test chamber, and they end up having some very...*interesting* conversations. They are one-sided conversations because, in the manner of most video game protagonists, Chell doesn't speak. Let's just say that it was a good thing that GLaDOS wasn't really interested in world domination.

Portal's success was so absolute that

the developers at Valve began work on a sequel immediately. Most video game sequels aren't as good as the first one, and the programming team for *Portal 2*—expanded from eight people to over thirty—were well aware of this. They worked hard and came up with a new game mechanic: spray-painting surfaces to alter their behavior. In combination with the portal gun from the first game, *Portal 2* would go on to become just as successful as *Portal*.

2009

MINECRAFT

THE WORLD IS YOUR SANDBOX

Markus "Notch" Persson worked as a game developer, but he learned many different programming languages in his free time. As a hobby, he would work on coding his own games at home.

Notch first developed the original edition of *Minecraft* in May 2009. *Minecraft* put players in a completely randomized world made up of different blocks. They could explore different environments and build items while trying to survive enemy "mobs" like zombies. He released a test video on YouTube, showing an early version of the game. The base program of *Minecraft* was finished over the space of a

> **DID YOU KNOW?**
> In the original version of the game, there were only seven mobs. Now, there are over 70!

single weekend and was released on some coding forums. Notch took feedback from other users on the forums and updated his game accordingly.

The first major update, "Alpha," was released on 30 June 2010. Notch had a day job, but he eventually quit so that he could work on *Minecraft* full-time. He continued to update the game with releases distributed automatically. The updates included new items, new blocks, new mobs, new game modes, and changes to the game's behavior. Notch eventually set up a video company, Mojang, with the money he was earning from the game.

Notch announced that *Minecraft* would enter beta-testing on 20 December 2010. He also stated that bug fixes and all updates leading up to and including the release would still be free—which has remained true

---

DID YOU KNOW?

Having trouble in the End Realm with all of those pesky Endermen? Here are a few tips to help you out:

- Wear a carved pumpkin on your head! For some reason, the Endermen can't tell if you're looking at them if you're wearing a carved pumpkin instead of a helmet. This really helps if you just want to run in, collect the stuff you dropped the last time you died, and get back out.
- Carry a bucket of water in your hotbar! Endermen don't like water at all, and they can't teleport into it. So, if you've got a whole group chasing you, pour out your water bucket and watch them all teleport away while you get a chance to get your health back up.
- Make an Enderman-free zone! Since Endermen are over two blocks tall, they can't fit into two-block high spaces like you can. If you build a little platform with a two-block gap beneath it, you can run underneath it and smack their ankles with your weapon of choice. Plus, it's a great way to get a lot of Ender Pearls!

---

throughout the entirety of *Minecraft*'s lifespan. The base game costs money (about $30 USD) but all updates and bug fixes remain free to this day.

Minecraft version 1.0 was released

on 18 November 2011 and is known as the "Adventure Update." Throughout the years, *Minecraft* has had the following updates:

- **Pre-Classic ("Cave Game")**—released May 10, 2009
  - Features: world generation, basic game mechanics, basic lighting, physics, particles

- **Classic**—released May 16, 2009
  - Features: an increased variety of blocks

- **Indev**—released December 23, 2009
  - Features: inventory space, crafting, dynamic lighting, diamonds, consumable food to restore health, tools, and equipment, day and night cycle

- **Infdev**—released February 27, 2010
  - Features: infinite map generation, 3D clouds, dynamic fluid system, complex cave systems

- **Alpha (Halloween Update)**—released June 30, 2010

- Features: survival multiplayer mode (SMP), The Nether, biomes, difficulty toggle

- **Beta (Adventure Update)**—released December 20, 2010
  - Features: new logo and launcher, achievements and statistics, creative mode, weather, updated lighting mechanics, improved graphical effects, naturally generated structures such as Strongholds, Abandoned Mineshafts, and Villages, beds for skipping through the night

- **Minecraft (official game)**—released November 18, 2011
- **1.0**— November 18, 2011
  - Features: hardcore mode, status effects, item repair, brewing, enchanting, breeding mobs, the End dimension, Nether Fortresses

> **DID YOU KNOW?**
>
> If you have pet parrots and you sit them down near a jukebox, they will do a wiggly dance to any music you play from the jukebox.

- **1.1**—January 12, 2012
  - Features: new languages, superflat worlds, changes to brewing and enchanting mechanics

- **1.2.1**—March 1, 2012
  - Features: jungle biome, iron golems, redstone lamps, ocelots

- **1.3.1**—August 1, 2012
  - Features: large biomes, adventure mode, villager trading, new commands, wooden slabs and stairs

- **1.4.2 (The Pretty Scary Update)**— October 25, 2012
  - Features: The Wither, Wither skeletons, witches, bats, carrots, potatoes, mob heads, flower pots, beacons

DID YOU KNOW?

For some materials, it's easier to make a farm to get more of them than it is to go out looking for them in the world. (It's also easier on your computer or game console.) Pumpkins and melons, cactus, sugarcane, bamboo, and even cobblestone can all be easily farmed with just a bit of redstone magic. You can find lots of tutorials on YouTube to teach you how.

- **1.5 (Redstone Update)**—March 13, 2013
  - Features: nether quartz, redstone blocks, comparators, pressure plates, hoppers, droppers, daylight sensors, new redstone mechanics

- **1.6 (The Horse Update)**—July 1, 2013
  - Features: horses, donkeys, mules, hay bales, terracotta and hardened clay blocks

- **1.7 (The Update That Changed The World)**— October 25, 2013
  - Features: new biomes (deep ocean, extreme hills+, mega taiga, taiga, flower forest,

birch forest, roofed forest, sunflower plains, savanna, and mesa), stained glass and stained glass panes, salmon, pufferfish, amplified world generation

- **1.8 (The Bountiful Update)**— September 2, 2014
  - Features: ocean monuments, prismarine blocks, sponge blocks, banners, guardians, elder guardians

- **1.9 (The Combat Update)**— February 29, 2016
  - Features: new types of arrows, changes to axe functionality, shields, dual-wielding items, igloos, End cities, Chorus Plant trees, elytra

- **1.10 (The Frostburn Update)**— June 8, 2016
  - Features: changes to the generation of "hot" and "cold" biomes, magma blocks, bone blocks, polar bears, strays, husks

- **1.11 (The Exploration Update)**—
  November 14, 2016
  - Features: woodland mansions, shulker boxes, totems of undying, Illagers, llamas

- **1.12 (The World of Color Update)**—
  June 7, 2017
  - Features: concrete, concrete powder, glazed terracotta, parrots

- **1.13 (The Update Aquatic)**— July 18, 2018
  - Features: dolphins, drowned zombies, tropical fish (up to 3072 different colors, patterns, and shapes), turtles, phantoms, tridents, coral blocks, kelp and seagrass, conduits, shipwrecks, underwater ruins, icebergs, coral reefs

- **1.14 (Village and Pillage)**— April 23, 2019
  - Features: updated villager trading functions, updated village generation based on

biome location, wandering traders, trader llamas, foxes, pandas, pillagers, ravagers, bamboo, scaffolding, lanterns, utility blocks, pillager outposts, crossbows, cats

- **1.15 (Buzzy Bees)**— December 10, 2019
  - Features: bees, honey bottles, honeycomb, bee nests, beehives, honey blocks

- **1.16 (Nether Update)**— June 23, 2020
  - Features: new biomes (soul sand valley, crimson forest, warped forest, basalt delta), bastion remnants, ruined portals

- **1.17 (Caves and Cliffs, Part**

1)— June 8, 2021
- Features: amethyst geodes, azalea trees, dripstone, moss, axolotls, goats, deepslate

- **1.18 (Caves and Cliffs, Part 2)**— November 30, 2021
  - Features: massive changes to world generation (including expanding world height limits down to Y: -64 and up to Y: 320), expanded cave generation ("cheese," "spaghetti," and "noodle" caves), deepslate generation below Y: 0, dripstone caves, lush caves, new mountain biomes (meadow, grove, snowy slopes, jagged peaks, frozen peaks, stony peaks), ore veins

- **Version 1.19 (The Wild Update)** has also been announced. It is currently available to play in beta-testing. It will include Deep Dark Cities and updates to the swamp biomes, as well as adding frogs and fireflies.

In 2014, Notch sold Mojang to Microsoft. To this day, *Minecraft* is the best-selling video game of all time. Over 238 million copies of the game have been sold, and in 2021, there were nearly 140 million active players each month.

DID YOU KNOW?

If you like Minecraft but just aren't sure how to build something, there are lots of great YouTubers and Twitch streamers who make tutorial videos.

- For redstone machines, check out MumboJumbo, docm77, or ilmango.
- For farms that get you lots and lots of items, look up ImpulseSV, TangoTek, or Shulkercraft.
- For building and terraforming tips, you can watch Grian, BdoubleO100, fWhip, GoodTimesWithScar, or GeminiTay.
- For general tips on how to play the game and how Minecraft works, you can learn from Pixlriffs or wattles.
- For information about updates to Minecraft, check out xisumavoid.

FIVE NIGHTS AT FREDDY'S

THE HORROR PHENOMENON THAT STARTED A NEW GENRE

RATED T FOR TEEN

In 2014, game developer Scott Cawthon released *Five Nights at Freddy's*. The premise of the game is pretty simple: you, the player, are an employee working overnight shifts at "Freddy Fazbear's Pizza," a family restaurant that has animatronic mascots (think the robotic characters you might see on amusement park rides). But the animatronics are coming to life on their own... and they are trying to kill you. Using only simple tools like flashlights, control panels, and security doors, it's your goal to survive the night and keep yourself safe.

So simple, and yet so successful. *Five*

Nights at Freddy's was an instant hit, and in the years since, no less than eight main sequels and a number of spinoff games were released to follow the story of the first game. In addition, developer Scott Cawthon has worked with fans of the FNaF series to develop officially recognized game series that are not sequels but are set in the same universe. These include *Five Nights at Flumpty's*, *Five Nights at Candy's*, *POPGOES*, and *The Joy of Creation* series. There are over twenty games in the entire "Fazbear Fanverse." Twenty games in only eight years is a lot of games! Other media, including novels and short stories, have also been published in the Fazbear Fanverse.

To be very clear, the *Five Nights at Freddy's* games are absolutely, definitely

---

DID YOU KNOW?

After a video of famous actor Jack Black dancing to one of the FNaF songs went viral on TikTok, he stated that he was a fan of the games. Later on, Jack Black even played some of the FNaF games with YouTuber Markiplier to promote his upcoming film *Goosebumps* (based on the children's horror books by R.L. Stine).

horror games. After all, the goal of the game is to survive each night until morning, and failure to do so will result in a well-timed jumpscare: Freddy, or one of his animatronic friends Bonnie, Chica, or Foxy, will pop up in the player's face with a screeching noise. There's no blood, but one of those jumpscares results in a game over, so you can pretty much assume that you've been killed.

Despite the fact that the *FNaF* games are horror games and rated T (the equivalent of a PG-13 movie), some of the biggest fans of the game are, in fact, kids. Other horror games with violence and disturbing graphics definitely don't have the same appeal for kids as they do for adults. But there's something about the *FNaF* games that younger gamers just find *cool*. Maybe it's just the thrill: most horror fans, after all, aren't in it for the blood and guts but for the shivers down their spines. Think of it like riding a roller coaster for the very first time: your heart was probably in your throat, and it was probably pretty scary; but in the end, it was wild and crazy and actually pretty fun. That's the kind of thrill that fans of the *FNaF* games seek out when they play the games.

One of the biggest reasons why fans love the games so much is the lore. Without spoiling too much of the story, all of the games are connected and have small easter eggs and details that connect them to one another. Sometimes, these details come in the form of 8-bit minigames, and sometimes they appear as voice messages from other characters in the game. Piece by piece, game by game, these details reveal a story that connects all the games together—and can be surprisingly sad and complex.

FNaF has had mixed reviews from critics, but fan reception has ultimately been highly positive, with each game selling millions of copies.

SPLATOON

A COMPETITIVE THIRD-PERSON SHOOTER...PLUS SQUID PEOPLE

RATED E10+ FOR EVERYONE 10+

Territory control games sound a little boring out of context, but the *Splatoon* series is anything but boring. You play as an "Inkling," a creature that can shift between a humanoid in order to hold weapons or a squid to hide or swim through ink. The weapons are used to shoot colorful ink onto surfaces and claim them as your territory; likewise, they damage your opponents and prevent them from claiming your territory.

Splatoon was released by Nintendo for the Wii U on May 28, 2015. It was well-received by the gaming community.

Territory control was a new genre for Nintendo, and critics in the industry agreed that they had done it really well. However, the game was criticized at the time for having a small number of multiplayer maps at launch and technical issues with online matches. Nintendo followed up on these criticisms by providing post-release support for the game, fixing bugs and adding new maps and weapons.

Nintendo also began holding limited-time events in the game called "Splatfests." Players are asked a binary question—meaning a question with only two answers—and take sides based on the answer they chose. Sometimes the questions were simple: do you prefer cats or dogs? Sometimes, they were more complicated: which came first, the chicken or the egg? The team that performed the most successfully during the event would receive better rewards at the end of it, but overall, the Splatfests didn't really affect the playability of the game...at least, not until the developers of the *Splatoon* games revealed that the last "Splatfest" for the first game affected the story of *Splatoon 2*. The question for that Splatfest had to do with the two protagonists of the story campaign, Marie and Callie. Players were simply asked to pick one and then play. Marie turned out to be the winner...and without spoiling the plot, that would be very important to the story of *Splatoon 2*, which was released in 2017 for the Nintendo Switch. *Splatoon 3* has also been announced and is set to release sometime in 2022 for the Nintendo Switch as well.

Because the *Splatoon* games have competitive game modes, they have become popular in esports tournaments. Up until 2018, the tournaments weren't official; but at that point, Nintendo stepped in and formally organized the *Splatoon 2 World Championships*. Teams of four could compete against one another in smaller qualifying tournaments or live tournaments in order to earn the right to play at the Nintendo World Championships. You might even be able to catch a livestream of the Nintendo World Championships during the annual E3 events and watch some of the most talented gamers in the world face off against one another!

The protagonists of the *Splatoon* series are fictional pop stars. They create and perform the music you hear in the game. In order to celebrate the success of one million copies of Splatoon sold, Nintendo held a concert tour for the group *Squid Sisters* in 2016; and they repeated the tour for *Off the Hook* in 2018. Obviously, the characters aren't real—so the concerts were virtual concerts and featured holograms of the protagonists projected onto glass panes to make them look three-dimensional!

ROCKET LEAGUE

IT'S NOT YOUR PARENTS' FIFA

RATED E FOR EVERYONE

R*ocket League* has a simple concept: it's soccer played by rocket-powered cars. Simple...yet brilliant.

You can have up to eight players on each team. The goal, as with regular soccer, is to hit the ball between the opponent's goalposts and score points. You can play in single-player or multiplayer, on the couch with your friends or online with distant cousins. In more recent updates, they've come up with rules based on ice hockey and basketball in addition to soccer.

One of the best parts about *Rocket League* is that the ball is almost comically

too large. If you're not driving quite fast enough when you hit it, it's possible to whiff it and have it just roll right over you. This doesn't damage you, but it's inconvenient given the general speed of gameplay. What *can* damage you is if your opponent rams you hard enough to destroy your car. You'll respawn... on your side of the field. You can even jump to hit the ball in mid-air. All of these features combine with the on-field speed boosts to create a game that is half soccer, and half...monster truck rally? Demolition derby? Illegal street drag racing? Those awesome robot fighting videos you get in your YouTube ads? Well, whatever it is, it's a ton of fun!

Rocket League was well-received by players and critics alike, as it was an improvement to an almost unknown prequel, *Supersonic Acrobatic Rocket-Powered Battle-Cars*. You can imagine why they changed the title, as that's...a bit of a mouthful.

Psyonix, the developers of *Rocket League*, have been among the most vocal supporters of cross-platform gaming. Makes sense: the game has been success-ful on every platform on which it has been released. *Rocket League* was orig-inally released for PlayStation 4 and Microsoft Windows in 2015 but has since been ported to Xbox One, PlayStation 4 Pro, and Nintendo Switch. These days, you can play *Rocket League* on any of these consoles, with any person playing on any other type of console. That's definitely something you couldn't have done in 2015!

Due to the popularity of *Rocket League* matches on livestreaming plat-forms such as Twitch, Psyonix decided to create an e-sports league. In March 2016, the company announced the first

Rocket League Championship series. The winners took home a $55,000 prize pool, and the championship earned over one million dollars in revenue—which went right back into further competitions. There's been a lot of prize money in Rocket League Championships, from college scholarships to a one-*million*-dollar prize in 2020.

Rocket League is one of many games that uses microtransactions for optional content, such as cosmetic items (aka "skins") and loot crates containing blueprints for new car models. Always be careful and responsible when playing a game that has microtransactions—make sure you have permission from your parents!

2015

UNDERTALE

THE POWER OF CHOICE

RATED E10+ FOR EVERYONE 10+

I n 2015, indie game developer Toby Fox published a little game called *Undertale*. On the surface, *Undertale* appears to be a simple game. You play as a child who has fallen into the Underground—the magical realm of monsters, separated from Earth by a barrier. Initially, of course, your goal is to get back to the surface. You're a child, and these are monsters! It's dangerous, and you would have no way to defend yourself!

But as it turns out...you don't have to defend yourself. You can fight, of course. There are ways to defeat monsters. But there are also ways to avoid fighting. You can run away, or you can try and talk to the monsters or calm them down. It all comes down to how you want to approach the game.

In most video games, our choices are very clear. As the playable character proceeds through the game, there are usually enemies, and you usually just defeat them and move on because you have to in order to complete the game. *Undertale* forces you to think about what you, as a person, are actually comfortable with doing. In real life, do you think you could kill a monster? In real life, would you try to run away, or calm the monster down? It's these kinds of choices in the game that have made *Undertale* so massively successful. The dialogue, characters, and the story of the game change depending on your choices—just like real life. It really makes you think about how your actions affect the people around you and

---

DID YOU KNOW?

In 2016, popular YouTuber MatPat visited the Vatican and even gave Pope Francis a copy of *Undertale*! According to MatPat, he gave Pope Francis the game because it represented the concept of "mercy" in an important way. Unfortunately, we'll never know if the Pope actually played it.

---

how what you say and do will affect your future.

But the open-ended morality system isn't the only reason for *Undertale's* success. Toby Fox, the developer of *Undertale*, made almost the entire game by himself. This includes the music, and *Undertale* is well known for its music. Perhaps you've heard of a little tune called "Megalovania"?

Of course, you can't forget the characters. From "goat mom" Toriel to Undyne, head of the royal guard; from Alphys, the royal scientist, to the iconic skeleton brothers Papyrus and Sans—each of these characters are unique, funny, and lovable. As you journey through the Underground, the player faces each of these characters and learns of their connection to the main story and is able to choose how they will interact with them. Perhaps this is one of the reasons why the choices in *Undertale* have made such an emotional impact on the game's fanbase: if you love the characters, it's hard to fight them.

Undertale was released for Microsoft Windows and OS X in September 2015, and it was later ported to Linux, PlayStation 4 and PlayStation Vita, the Nintendo Switch, and Xbox One. It has sold over one million copies and is regarded as one of the best games of the 2010s.

ORI AND THE BLIND FOREST

THE POWER OF FAMILY

RATED E FOR EVERYONE

Ori and the Blind Forest was developed by Moon Studios and published by Microsoft Studios, and it was released for Xbox One and Microsoft Windows in March 2015 as well as Nintendo Switch in 2019.

Ori and the Blind Forest will *immediately* hook you with storytelling. The game uses magnificent art and animation alongside beautiful music and sound design to help players understand what is going on with barely any words used at all. You play as Ori, a small spirit of light who resembles a...monkey. Or a fox. Or a Pokémon. Whatever he is, he's cute. And almost immediately, you are introduced to Ori's adopted mother,

Naru. At first, Naru might look at bit menacing, especially if you've watched the Studio Ghibli film *Spirited* Away. She looks a little bit like the character No-Face. But then you learn that Naru is actually a really great mom, and Ori is really cute, and they are a small happy family doing their best until...well...

...well, it wouldn't be a video game if tragedy didn't strike *somewhere*, would it?

Without spoiling the game too much, let's just say Ori has to go on a journey. Along the way, he meets Sein, a spirit who introduces herself as "the light and eyes of the Spirit Tree." Sein helps Ori to gain new powers, such as shooting fireballs and performing double and triple jumps—abilities that are absolutely vital in a platformer game like *Ori and the Blind Forest*.

Throughout the game, the player is treated to more breathtaking visuals and audio. The colors of the game are bright and beautiful (except when they aren't supposed to be), and according to Moon Studios developer and artist Thomas Mahler, all of the background art pieces (often referred to as "assets") are individually designed, with no duplicates. Video games often duplicate trees or rocks or mushrooms so that they only have to design one or two to copy into new locations. This is generally easier on both the game code and the artists. But Moon Studios wanted a very hand-drawn, dreamy feeling in the art of *Ori and the Blind Forest* and decided to create each asset by hand. The music is also stellar, with fully orchestrated themes for different areas of the game that fade flawlessly into one another as Ori moves from place to place. The company put a great deal of hard work and care into *Ori and the Blind Forest*, and it really shows.

When *Ori and the Blind Forest* was released, it was immediately successful—becoming profitable for both Microsoft Studios *and* Moon Studios within a few weeks of release, which is rare for indie games.

Ori and the Will of the Wisps, an immediate sequel, was announced in 2017 and released in March 2020 for Xbox One and Microsoft Windows, in September 2020 for Nintendo Switch, and in November 2020 for the Xbox Series X/S as its launch title. It was just as well-received as the first game. Both *Ori and the Blind Forest* and *Ori and the Will of the Wisps* have won awards for their art, music, game design, and storytelling.

HOLLOW KNIGHT

SAVE THE WORLD... BUT AT WHAT COST?

RATED E10+ FOR EVERYONE 10+

I n *Hollow Knight*, you play as the Knight, a small bug of indeterminate species (though based on the mask, they may just be a beetle). The Knight arrives in the kingdom of Hallownest, inhabited by other bugs who are both friendly and hostile, and explores to gain new abilities, learn about their past, and ultimately determine the fate of the entire kingdom.

The aesthetic of *Hollow Knight* is both creepy and cute. All of the characters resemble some kind of insect, but they're drawn so simply—or wearing masks and cloaks—that they don't really look that scary. The background art of the game is dark and a little bit moody, and the music, for the most part, is very calming... until you accidentally wander into a boss fight, that is.

The gameplay seems simple at first glance. *Hollow Knight* is a Metroidvania platformer, and the Knight has the Nail (a melee weapon similar to a sword) to defend themselves with. Over time, the Knight gains access to healing abilities, spells, and movement abilities such as dashing, wall jumping, and double jumping. The difficulty lies in actually getting those abilities because *Hollow Knight* is a fairly difficult game, for all its creepy-cute looks.

Hollow Knight is interesting in that there are multiple ways to get to pretty much every location in the game—and almost all of the areas in the game are optional. This has resulted in a large speedrunning community among the *Hollow*

Knight fanbase, with the most common category being "any%, no major glitches." The world record in this category as of February 2022 is held by a user named "pest," who completed the game in just thirty-two minutes and sixteen seconds.

Hollow Knight was well-received by audiences after its release by three-man indie game developer company, Team Cherry. *Hollow Knight* was praised for requiring the player to be patient and practice certain types of skills, such as "spike pogos" (using the Nail to bounce off spikes without taking damage, to gain extra movement ability) or "acid skips" (using a mid-game super-dash ability to get across a pond of acid without gaining the ability that would allow the player to simply swim in the acid). Many players also enjoyed the sense of satisfaction gained after defeating particularly tricky boss fights—especially if they had died several times to that boss.

Team Cherry, the developers of *Hollow Knight*, have also contributed to the success of the game by continuing to create massive amounts of content and free DLC following the initial release of the game. In an age where most game companies put small amounts of DLC behind a paywall to get more money out of the customers, it's gratifying for a game of such excellent quality as *Hollow Knight* to provide so much more for free. And *Hollow Knight* isn't even that expensive to begin with—it only costs about $15 USD on any of the game platforms: PC, macOS, Linux, Nintendo Switch, PlayStation 4, and Xbox One. *Hollow Knight* has sold over 2.8 million copies so far; and a sequel, *Silksong*, was announced in 2019 but has not yet been released.

FORTNITE

BE THE LAST PERSON
STANDING IN A
HUNDRED-PLAYER
BATTLE ROYALE...
AND MORE

RATED T FOR TEEN

In 2017, the company Epic Games released an online video game called *Fortnite*. It was almost an overnight hit, gathering more than 125 million players in less than a year and earning hundreds of millions of dollars per month!

There are three game modes in *Fortnite*. They are *Fortnite: Save the World*, *Fortnite Battle Royale*, and *Fortnite Creative*.

In *Fortnite: Save the World*, players cooperate with one another to fight

DID YOU KNOW?

Some of the best-known Fortnite dances are Best Mates, Floss, The Robot, Emote 4 Fresh, Disco Fever, Tidy, Ride the Pony, and Wiggle.

DID YOU KNOW?

Most Fortnite skins are designed by the Epic Games staff designers, but more recently, Fortnite has had skin design competitions called "Concept Royale." During a Concept Royale, players and artists all around the world are invited to submit ideas for new Fortnite skins, and those that are chosen will make it into the game. If you've got a great idea for a Fortnite skin, maybe someday we'll all see it in the game!

off zombies, collect data on a mysterious apocalyptic storm, and defend objects by building traps and fortifications.

In *Fortnite Creative*, players are given complete freedom to create worlds and battle arenas. It has been compared to Minecraft's creative mode and other sandbox games such as *Terraria*, *Roblox*, and *Creativerse*.

However, when most people think of *Fortnite*, they

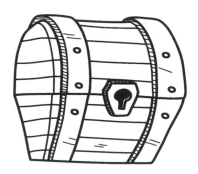

think of *Fortnite Battle Royale*. In *Battle Royale* mode, up to one hundred players fight against one another to be the last person standing. Players airdrop from a "Battle Bus" that crosses the selected map. When the players land, they must scavenge for weapons, items, and resources and compete to survive. As the game progresses, the map shrinks to force players to encounter one another. The last player remaining wins the game.

AMONG US

WHEN THE IMPOSTER IS SUS

RATED E10+ FOR EVERYONE 10+

You've seen the videos, you've laughed at the memes. Everyone knows about *Among Us*, especially because the game's popularity skyrocketed during the COVID-19 pandemic. Groups of YouTubers and Twitch streamers got together and played this funny little game, and the internet went wild for it.

Among Us is what's known as a "social deduction" game. Most social deduction games are party games, meaning that you're supposed to play them with groups of people in-person. The most popular version of the party game is *Mafia*, though there are also variations such as *Werewolf*; there are

even other video games based on the concept of this game, such as *Town of Salem*.

The premise of the game, online or not, is fairly simple: in a group of people, a few are selected as impostors (or mafia, or werewolves). The goal of the

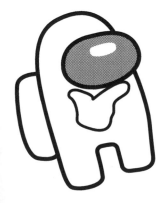

impostors is to elimi-
nate the other players;
the goal of the other
players is to figure out
who the impostors are
and eliminate them first.
Among Us took the game to
a whole new level by
theming it around space,
astronauts, and aliens.
One of the creators
of *Among Us*, Marcus
Bromander, even said
that he was inspired
by the science horror
fiction film *The Thing*
while making *Among Us*.

> **DID YOU KNOW?**
> *Among Us* wasn't originally named Among Us. Because the game is a space-themed version of Mafia/Werewolf, it was originally named "SpaceMafia."

    Among Us was released
in 2018 but didn't do
well financially until
mid-2020. COVID-19 is sometimes cited as
the reason for the popularity of the
game because it allows for socialization despite social distancing. However,
coverage by popular YouTubers and Twitch
streamers is equally likely to have contributed to that popularity.
    The best way to play *Among Us* is with

> **DID YOU KNOW?**
>
> If you change your computer or console date to April 1, all of the maps will be backward. If you change your computer or console date to October 31 or December 25, you'll get appropriately holiday-themed hats for your crewmate/impostor to wear as you complete your tasks.

a group of people you already know. You or one of your friends can host a private game on the game's interface, then send a key to the people you want to invite to the game. It's more fun to play with people you know because social deduction games rely on making decisions about what other people are saying and doing. It's easier (and safer) to do that with friends than with strangers!

GLOSSARY

CAN YOU MASTER
THESE TERMS?

Easter eggs: You've probably heard the term, but on the off chance that you haven't, an Easter egg is a reference or a joke included in a game for players to find for fun. One of the most infamous (and early) examples of an Easter egg is in Atari's *Adventure*.

Farm: A "farm" in gaming is an easy and repetitive action (sometimes known as an "exploit") that allows players to obtain items or experience points/level-ups quickly. This is often done to prevent the game's main story from progressing before the player achieves the goal they want.

Gacha: Gacha games are mobile games

where opening chests and obtaining loot is the key way of unlocking characters and furthering the game. This is usually done with an in-game currency. The term "gacha" comes from the "gashapon" vending machine games popular in Japan. *Genshin Impact* is one of the most popular examples of a gacha game, but there are a lot out there!

....

Hotbar: A hotbar is basically a row of buttons. It is often used as a gameplay mechanic that gives the player easy access to certain abilities they use throughout the game. On PC (computer) games, the hotbar is most commonly accessed by pressing the keys 1-0 and is usually customizable!

....

Massively Multiplayer Online Game (MMO): An MMO is an online game with a huge player base. This can range from the hundreds of thousands to even the millions! For example, *World of Warcraft* is an MMO with millions of players. A popular form of MMO is an MMORPG, meaning that they are RPGs that have a massive online player base.

Metroidvania: Metroidvania games are a type of game inspired by early *Castlevania* and *Metroid* games, blending the action and exploration elements of both franchises. Backtracking through levels to unlock new areas is a common feature of Metroidvanias. Usually, these games are two-dimensional, open-world, side-scrolling platformer games.

Not Rated Skin: In video gaming, a skin is an item or a customization option in a game that allows you to change the physical appearance of your character. One skin might give you a new outfit while another can change your entire look or even species!

Open world: A game that has an open world is all about exploration! Instead of following a strict, linear story, open world games allow the player to complete objectives whenever they see fit. The world is freely available to the player; anywhere you want to go

in the game can be traveled to at any
time.

....

Platformer: A platformer game puts the
player in a series of levels in which
they have to traverse…you guessed it.
Platforms. Players have to run and jump
through different environments, usually
avoiding enemies and falls along the
way. Along with the obvious *Mario*
games, the *Kirby* games are a popular
example.

....

Role Playing Game (RPG): Similar
to sandbox games, RPGs give the
player a huge space to explore
and a large amount of control over
their experience. However, character
customization is a key feature of an
RPG. It's supposed to feel like *you* are
that character. The player character
unlocks new abilities or items as the
game progresses. Sometimes this can
take the form of different "classes"
for the player to choose from and
"skill points" to help a character
level up. For instance, if you are a

"mage" class, you can probably use a lot of powerful spells. RPGs also tend to have developed worlds packed full of non-player characters ("NPCs") that the players can interact with. There are many different kinds of RPGs (like Action RPGs or Strategy RPGs). *The Elder Scrolls* series (particularly *Skyrim*) and *Mass Effect* series are both examples of popular ARPGs.

Sandbox: Sandbox games are centered around creativity—a player is given a large space to play in (the "sandbox") and many different options for exploring, building on, or destroying the space. A popular example of this is *Minecraft*—which sometimes literally places you in a "sandbox" desert environment.

Side-scrolling: A side-scrolling game is a type of game that has a camera fixed in a side view, following the player's movements left and right. Games like *Super Mario Bros.*, *Donkey Kong Country*, and even *Cuphead* are considered side-scrollers.

Social deduction games: Social deduction games are games in which players are placed on opposing sides but are unaware of who is on what side. The players (usually those on a "good" side) have to deduce (or figure out) who is on their side before they are eliminated.

Soulsborne: A Soulsbourne game is a type of game that is methodical and requires concentration and focus (usually in combat). These games are famous for being difficult and punishing. The name stems from the two FromSoftware series of games that popularized this style of gameplay— *Souls* and *Bloodborne*.

Table Top Game (TTG): Although not a video game, this is a type of game that has influenced a lot of video games. TTGs are played by a group of friends around a table (hence the name "table top"). TTGs are also often RPGs, leading to the common phrase "TTRPG," though some table top games can be strategy games. Players can play TTRPGs for multiple sessions that last for hours. It's a lot like playing pretend with a group of people! The most popular example of this is *Dungeons & Dragons*, which can be seen in the popular Netflix series *Stranger Things*.

Territory control: Territory control games (or "area control games") are competitive games/game modes that involve teams of players fighting over specific sections and points on a map. Put simply, you have a specific territory that you need to control.

About the Author

S.E. Abramson graduated from Brigham Young University in 2016 with a BA in English. She lives in south-central Pennsylvania with her family. She enjoys writing, video games, and anthroponomastics.

About Bushel & Peck Books

Bushel & Peck Books is a children's publishing house with a special mission. Through our Book-for-Book Promise™, we donate one book to kids in need for every book we sell. Our beautiful books are given to kids through schools, libraries, local neighborhoods, shelters, nonprofits, and also to many selfless organizations that are working hard to make a difference. So thank you for purchasing this book! Because of you, another book will make its way into the hands of a child who needs it most.

Nominate a School or Organization to Receive Free Books

Do you know a school, library, or organization that could use some free books for their kids? We'd love to help! Please fill out the nomination form on our website (see below), and we'll do everything we can to make something happen.

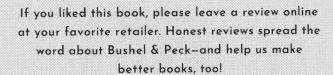

www.bushelandpeckbooks.com/pages/
nominate-a-school-or-organization

If you liked this book, please leave a review online at your favorite retailer. Honest reviews spread the word about Bushel & Peck—and help us make better books, too!